CONTENTS

To Anna, Emily, Deborah, Andrew and Paul

1 The First Day

Sarah and Paul MacDonald are twins. The day they had been waiting for had arrived at last - the first day of their holidays. For weeks they had been thinking of things to do and places to explore.

On their birthday earlier that year, they had bought new suitcases with their birthday money. Their excitement grew as they decided what to take with them on holiday. They were going to a cabin by the sea. Changing their minds frequently as to what to take, they had packed and unpacked their suitcases, and packed them again lots of times!

But now they had arrived at the holiday cabin. They unpacked their suitcases, although not very carefully, and put their things where they wanted them in their rooms.

Paul finished first and went to find Sarah. 'Have you finished, Sarah?'

'Yes, let's get Dad to take us down to the beach.'

'A good idea!' agreed Mrs MacDonald, coming into Sarah's room. 'If Dad takes you out, it will give me a chance to get the lunch ready, and to unpack our things - besides tidying up your rooms.' She said the last words with a smile, because she shared the twins' excitement about the beginning of the holidays.

'It'll be good when we can go into the water,' exclaimed Sarah, as she saw people in their swimsuits walking along the beach.

'I want to collect shells this year,' added Paul.

Sarah was on the point of saying the same when she asked, 'What's that noise, Dad? It sounds like people singing on the beach.'

'Look!' said Mr MacDonald, pointing to a notice. 'There's been a beach mission for children going on all this week. This morning is the last meeting. Would you like to go? You've missed the games, but you'll be in time for most of the service.'

'Yes, please,' cried Sarah and Paul.

The sound of the singing led the twins and their father to the place where the service was being held. Crowds of children were sitting around a sand platform, made in the shape of a boat. Lots of parents were sitting where they could listen too. The leader of the mission was conducting the singing of choruses and a member of his team played the guitar.

One of the team members spotted Sarah

and Paul arriving and quickly came forward to welcome them and to find them a place where they could both see and hear. 'I'll come back at twelve,' whispered Mr MacDonald.

* * *

Lunch was late that day and, by the time they had finished the dishes, the weather had changed and it was no longer sunny.

'We'll go for a ride in the country,' said Mr MacDonald. 'Let's just take any road that looks interesting and explore it. We'll get lost, if you like!'

'Could you really get lost?' asked Paul, as they began to travel down a beautiful country road.

'Not really, Paul. We could lose our way easily enough, but it would be difficult to get really lost, especially with our new book of maps.'

Sarah was looking out of the car window. 'Look, that road looks exciting. May we explore that one, Dad?'

Before Sarah had finished her sentence, Mr MacDonald turned the car up the road. The narrow road twisted and turned, and in places the trees touched one another so much at the top that they shut out most of the light.

8

While they were driving along Mrs MacDonald asked the twins to tell her about the beach mission service.

'Well,' explained Sarah, 'because it was the last morning, the leader spoke about becoming a Christian and the wrong ideas people have about becoming a Christian. I'm sorry we missed the other services. There won't be any next week.'

'Me, too,' agreed Paul. 'That man could play the guitar well.'

The twins' parents smiled. 'I know what we could do then,' suggested Mr MacDonald. 'I've promised to speak to the Sunday School when we get back. I want to talk about how to become a Christian and what it means to follow the Lord Jesus. Suppose we talk about it together and then take some colour slides to illustrate what we learn?'

'What do you mean, Dad?' asked Sarah.

'We'll talk about what it means to be a Christian. Then, if we can, we'll make a note of things we can take photographs of and show people, to help them understand. You two could even write a script, which you could read and make a tape recording to go with the slides.'

'It sounds like fun!' cried Paul excitedly.

'Can we start now?'

'All right, Sarah. I've got paper and a pencil in the glove compartment. I'll stop the car and we'll work on this together. Let's think first about those wrong ideas you were hearing of this morning.'

Mr MacDonald wrote at the top of his page, 'You don't become a Christian by - '

'Where do we start?'

Sarah began. 'You don't become a Christian by going to church.'

Mr MacDonald drew a church and then he sketched in people with wind-up keys sticking out of their backs.

'You're right, Sarah,' he said, as he finished his drawing. 'People can go to church as regular as clockwork, out of habit, never really being Christians.'

'But Christians want to go to church, don't they, Dad?' asked Paul.

'Yes, they do. But just going to church isn't good enough. It does not make you a Christian. What else do some people think makes them Christians?'

'Being christened or baptised?' suggested Paul.

Mr MacDonald drew a minister sprinkling

a baby's forehead with water. He also drew another minister about to baptise an older person.

Paul was thinking about the photographs. 'It will be difficult to take a photograph of a baby or a grown-up being baptised.'

His father nodded in agreement. 'Yes, but we may have the opportunity. If not, we'll manage without.'

'Don't you become a Christian until you're baptised?' asked Sarah, puzzled.

'Some people may think so,' explained Mr MacDonald. 'But just going into the water, or having water sprinkled on your head, doesn't make you a Christian. Something much more important has to happen.'

'But if you're a Christian, you do want to be baptised, don't you?' asked Sarah.

'Yes, you do, because the Lord Jesus commanded that His followers should obey Him by being baptised. Now, is there anything else you know about which people may think makes you a Christian?'

'Having Christian parents,' Paul said. 'The man said so this morning.'

'That's right,' agreed Mr MacDonald, 'but I don't think I'll draw a picture of myself. I

11

know what we'll do.'

He drew a family sitting at a dining table, with their heads bowed, having family prayers.

'Because Mum and I are Christians, does that make you both Christians?'

'No,' the twins replied together.

'That's the right answer,' said their mother. 'Much as I would love you both to be Christians like Dad and me, I cannot make you Christians.'

'What about praying?' asked Sarah.

'Yes. People sometimes think that because they say their prayers God is pleased with them and He accepts them as Christians, but they're wrong.'

'The same is true of reading the Bible then,' added Paul.

Mr MacDonald nodded and drew matchstick men praying and reading the Bible. 'All Christians are meant to discover the importance of praying and reading the Bible, but these two things don't make anyone a Christian. Now I think we've come to the end almost. Is there anything else?'

'I know!' said Sarah. 'What about doing your best to help people?'

By the side of the matchstick men, praying and reading, the twins' father drew a boy carrying an old lady's shopping bag.

'Now remember,' he urged, 'it's important for Christians to help other people all they can and to do all the good they can. But trying to be good isn't the same as being a Christian.'

Mr MacDonald looked at the drawings critically. 'Not very good, I'm afraid.'

'They're not bad,' commented Paul sympathetically.

'They help you to remember things, anyway,' said Sarah.

'Good,' answered Mr MacDonald. 'When we take our photos, one of you could kneel to pray and the other one could read the Bible.'

'Don't forget the script,' Mrs MacDonald reminded her husband.

'Oh, yes. Who wants to do the script for the first pictures we're going to take?'

'I will,' offered Sarah.

'All right, girls first, I suppose,' said Paul.

2   The Top of Orchard Hill

After lunch on Sunday, Sarah was sitting at the dining room table writing and her mother sat on the opposite side doing the same.

'What are you writing about, Sarah?' asked Paul.

'I'm preparing the script and the drawings about what Dad said to us yesterday.'

'Let me see what you've written.'

'Not until I've finished, please,' pleaded Sarah. 'My drawings aren't very good.'

'You'll let me see, won't you, Sarah?' enquired her father.

'Well, all right, you may all look.'

'That's good!' exclaimed Paul, as he held up a rather amusing picture of a boy going to church with a wind-up key sticking out of his back.

'You know what we could do, Sarah?' suggested Mr MacDonald. 'If we can't always take a satisfactory photograph to illustrate what I want to tell the Sunday School, I can try to take a photograph of one of your drawings - that is, if the drawing is bold and clear enough.'

'May I try too, Dad?' asked Paul.

'Of course. But what about a walk now?

14

You've been sitting most of this morning, both in Sunday School and at church. As we're so near the country, we ought to make the most of it.'

Mrs MacDonald looked up from her writing. 'Do you mind, David,' she asked her husband, 'if I stay and finish my letters?'

'That's all right,' agreed Mr MacDonald. 'I'll get some paper and a pencil, in case we want to do any drawings. I think we'd better take our raincoats with us too. It looks like it could rain.'

It took the twins and their father about a quarter of an hour to get away from all the houses, out into the country. They had to cross a large main road, full of traffic, taking people to the various beaches along the coast.

'Let's find the best place to cross!' urged Mr MacDonald. 'If we cross over here at this island, we can go down that country road opposite. There won't be much traffic down there, and we can enjoy the walk without worrying about cars so much.'

They had to wait several minutes before there was a gap in the traffic. Then they hurried across and took the first turn on the left, which was a beautiful, winding country road.

'Isn't this lovely!' exclaimed Sarah. 'Do

15

you think we'll pass some farms, Dad?'

'I'm sure we will and there are some orchards along here too.'

'Look, there they are!' shouted Paul, pointing ahead of them on the left-hand side.

Tree after tree seemed to be laden with shiny red apples.

'That gives me an idea for what I'm going to talk to you about presently.'

'What?'

'Wait and see, Paul!' answered his father with a smile. 'Let's take this narrow road to the left which leads up to the top of Orchard Hill. It's a popular place. I expect we'll find quite a few people up there.'

There were two ways up. There was a long path which went round the side of the hill, gradually leading to the top. There was also a path straight up the hill, with a zigzag pattern of foot holes, by which one could climb up more quickly.

'Which way up?'

'Oh, the hard way, Dad!' shouted Paul.

'All right,' said his father, pretending to groan with disappointment. 'I'm ready.'

As they neared the top, the twins looked around and laughed at their father. 'Come on,

Dad, you're an old slow coach!'

'It's all right for you two. You're at the top. There's more of me to carry up the hill than there is of you!'

Mr MacDonald sat down on the stone seat at the top. 'Phew, I'm warm,' he said. 'Let's sit down for a moment and find out what we can see from up here.'

'That's the sea over there,' said Paul, pointing.

'And there's the main road we crossed,' added Sarah. 'You can see the road we came up too. It does look narrow, and see how it twists and winds.'

'Look at the cars and the people - they look like ants!' cried Paul.

Mr MacDonald placed a sheet of paper on the middle of the stone seat and brought out a pencil.

'Are you ready now, Paul, to remember things for your part of the script? From up here I can see a few things that will help me to explain something more of what it means to be a Christian.'

'I'm ready.'

'Me, too,' added Sarah.

'Well, do you both see the broad road we

crossed over?'

'Yes,' replied Sarah, 'and I just pointed out the small narrow road we turned into.'

'I'll draw them on this piece of paper.'

'Why, Dad?' asked Paul.

'The Lord Jesus said there are two roads in life.   There's a broad road which leads to disaster - that is, away from God and to what the Bible calls hell - and there are many people going that way.'

'Like all the cars and all the people travelling on that road?' interrupted Sarah.

Mr MacDonald nodded.   'And then the Lord Jesus said there's a narrow road which is much harder to travel on, leading to everlasting life and heaven.   And only a few people find that road.   Now watch carefully.'

On the broad road, he wrote, 'Paul was born here,' and underneath he wrote, 'Sarah was born here.'

'We're all born on the broad road,' explained the twins' father.   'And we deserve to remain on it because of our sinfulness and disobedience to God.   We certainly don't deserve to go on the narrow road which leads to heaven.   Now watch.'

At the place where the narrow road joined

the broad road in the drawing, Mr MacDonald drew a cross. 'God loved us so much,' he continued, 'that He sent the Lord Jesus into the world to die for our sins and to take the punishment that we deserve. Because the Lord Jesus died for sinners, God can forgive our sins when we are really sorry about them, and trust in the Lord Jesus as our Saviour. That's how we can leave the broad road and join the narrow. So becoming a Christian is leaving the broad road - on which most people are to be found - and going on the narrow road.'

Stopping for a moment, Mr MacDonald pointed. 'Look down there, twins.'

'Where, Dad?'

'To the orchards, Paul. When we walked by, did you notice if all the apples trees had good fruit on them?'

'Some were better than others,' answered Sarah. 'I saw one tree that wasn't nearly as good as the others. The leaves and the apples were all blotchy.'

'The Lord Jesus said that our lives are like trees,' explained Mr MacDonald. 'There are good trees and bad trees. Every good tree produces good fruit, but a bad tree produces bad fruit.'

Under the two roads on his piece of paper, he drew two trees. One had lots of apples on it. The other had little fruit on it, and the fruit was marked with spots. 'Let me ask you a question. When the fruit of a tree's bad, what's wrong?'

'I suppose something's wrong with the tree itself.'

'That's right, Sarah.'

Mr MacDonald drew two matchstick men and he drew hearts in the middle of them. One heart was black and the other was white. 'The wrong things that you and I do come from our hearts which are deceitful and often so full of wrong thoughts. The Bible says that our heart is black, like the heart of this man here,' he said, pointing to the black heart. 'What happens if you catch a cold?'

'You begin to sneeze.'

'Yes,' said Paul, 'and you get hot.'

'And your nose runs.'

'Correct,' agreed their father. 'These things begin to happen outside because of what's happening inside you. You and I sin because we've sin in our hearts. It's the sin in our hearts that makes us do wrong things.'

'That means we're all bad trees then,'

concluded Sarah.

'Yes, we are, because we're all born with hearts that are sinful. The important thing to learn is how our hearts can be made clean.'

'I suppose by asking Jesus to come into them,' said Paul.

'Yes, because His blood was shed on the cross to make our hearts clean,' added Sarah.

'Right,' said her father. 'The Bible compares this to two countries or two kingdoms. Look, I'll draw two crowns.'

Inside one crown Mr MacDonald wrote the word Satan and inside the other he wrote Jesus. 'The Bible says there's one king who reigns over our soul. Who do you think that king should be?'

Paul spoke first, 'Jesus.'

'Yes. He's our King if we're on the narrow road, and if we've let Him make us good trees. But what if we're not?'

'Then we are still in Satan's kingdom,' replied Paul.

Mr MacDonald drew some more matchstick men underneath the two crowns. 'Which kingdom do you feel I should draw more people under?'

'Satan,' suggested Paul, thoughtfully.

'Is that right, Sarah? When it comes to people's lives, as God sees them, are there more good trees than bad, or the other way around?'

'There are more bad, Dad.'

Her father thought for a moment. 'That brings us back to the same question as before: How can we leave Satan's kingdom? You watch me as I draw. We're on a hill, so I'll draw two hills, almost next to one another. One is Satan's kingdom and the other is the Lord Jesus' kingdom. How are we going to get across to the Lord Jesus' from Satan's? Will going to church do? Or trying our best?'

'No. Only trusting in the Lord Jesus,' said Sarah.

Mr MacDonald drew a cross between the two hills, which made a bridge over from one to the other. 'The Lord Jesus died on the cross to make a way for us to leave Satan's kingdom and to belong to His kingdom. Now let's see if you've understood. Becoming a Christian is like what, Sarah?' He pointed to the two roads.

'It's leaving the broad road and joining the narrow.'

'Next, Paul,' said the twins' father, pointing to the trees.

'It's stopping being a bad tree and

beginning to become a good tree.'

'Now you, Sarah.'

'It's stopping belonging to Satan's kingdom and belonging to Jesus instead.'

'Good!' said Mr MacDonald. 'Now, the question I would like to ask you is, which road are you on? What kind of tree are you? Which kingdom do you belong to? What about you, Paul?'

'I think I'm on the broad road, Dad,' he answered seriously.

'Which one do you want to be on, Paul?'

Paul had no doubt. 'I want to be on the narrow.'

'What about you, Sarah?'

'I think I may be upon the narrow, but I'm not sure.'

'Do you want to be sure?'

'Yes, I do,' answered Sarah quietly, looking at the drawings.

'Well, as we go on in our talks,' promised Mr MacDonald, 'and we see all that it means to become a Christian, I know God will help you both to be sure. When I speak to you about this again tomorrow, remind me to tell you about Michael Tenney and the time he was at camp.'

'Won't you tell us now?' pleaded Paul.

'No, I'll keep it until tomorrow,' answered his father, with a twinkle in his eye. 'I'll race you down the hill!'

'You wouldn't dare, Dad.'

'Wouldn't I, Sarah? Then here goes!'

Quickly but cautiously he started making his way down the hill, only to fall flat on his back.

'You can laugh,' shouted Mr MacDonald. 'I'll beat you down there yet.'

And he did!

3   Missing the Mark

'It's too bad you have to stay in to do the washing, Mum!' exclaimed Sarah, when she discovered that her mother had decided that she couldn't come out with them on that Monday morning.

'Well, you would look dirty at the end of the holidays if I didn't do any washing, wouldn't you?' replied her mother with a laugh. 'But it's not only because of the washing that I'm not going with you now. There are two or three letters I want to write and I can do that more easily if I'm here on my own for a while.'

It was decided that the twins and their father would walk to the beach, leaving the car with their mother so that she could join them after she had finished the washing and writing her letters.

Seeing the twins' disappointment, Mr MacDonald said, 'As a treat, twins, we'll get Mum to meet us at a restaurant and we'll have lunch out. How would that be?'

'Great,' said Paul. 'We hardly ever go out to a restaurant.'

'That'll be a treat for me too,' commented Mrs MacDonald. 'It means I won't have to make lunch and do dishes afterwards. So off you go! Here's an apple each for you to put in your pockets.'

The sun shone and there was a gentle breeze as Mr MacDonald and the twins walked leisurely to the beach.

'Dad, you promised to tell us about Michael Tenney and the time he went to camp,' Paul reminded his father.

'So I did,' exclaimed Mr MacDonald. 'I was only about sixteen and was still at school. Matthew Tenney, Michael's father, had invited me to help at his children's camp down in the country. It was the first time I'd been to a camp where we lived in tents. Every evening we had camp prayers and I took my turn at speaking to the boys and girls. I took some pictures and illustrations with me. One evening after supper, Michael, who was about eight or nine, came into my tent. I was getting ready for my talk at prayers and had some pictures of Zacchaeus on my bed. Do you remember the story of Zacchaeus?'

'Yes,' said Sarah. 'He was a cheat and he discovered that Jesus knew all about him.'

'Can you remember what he did?'

'Yes,' said Paul, 'he repented of his sins and

27

the Lord Jesus forgave him and gave him a new start in life.'

'Well, I talked to Michael about the story I was going to tell,' continued Mr MacDonald. 'I told him I was going to explain how we all need to be sorry for the things which we have done wrong and to ask the Lord Jesus to forgive us, and to become our Saviour.'

'What happened to Michael then?' asked Sarah.

'I said to Michael, "Has the Lord Jesus forgiven you your sins?" He said, "No." So I said, "Do you want Him to do so?" And he said, "Yes." So I explained what he needed to do, how that he had to confess his sins to God, to be sorry for them, and not to want to do them anymore. Then he must trust the Lord Jesus as his Saviour and receive Him into his life.'

'Did he do that?' asked Sarah seriously.

'Yes, we knelt by my bed, and Michael asked the Lord Jesus to be his Saviour and to cleanse his heart from sin. He wasn't very old, as I said, but he went and told his parents, who were glad because they had been praying that Michael would understand the Bible and become a Christian.' The twins' father paused for a moment. 'Which road had Michael left,

Sarah?'

'He had left the broad road and joined the narrow.'

'How was I to know that he had?'

'Because he told you so, I suppose,' said Paul.

'No, he might not really have meant it. How do you think he showed that he meant it?'

'By telling his parents?' suggested Paul.

'Yes. Any other way?'

'By the things he did and the way he behaved?' asked Sarah.

'Most of all by that, Sarah,' agreed Mr MacDonald. 'Michael has grown a lot as a Christian and this year he's helping in a beach mission like the one we saw on Saturday. He's now helping others to become Christians. But Michael had to learn for himself first of all what was wrong with him - he had to learn about his sin. And that's where we all have to begin.'

* * *

At one o'clock the twins and their father met their mother outside the restaurant they had chosen. Paul peered at the menu in the window.

'Yum, yum,' he said. 'I'm going to have a hamburger, and a strawberry milk shake.'

At the next table to the MacDonalds sat an elderly man. He watched the MacDonalds as they waited for the waitress to bring their orders.

'How nice and well behaved your children are,' the man said.

Mr MacDonald laughed and replied, 'Thank you very much.' Then he turned to the twins and said teasingly in a half whisper, 'People don't know how horrible you can be, do they?'

Sarah and Paul felt very grown-up eating in a restaurant, and they were on their best behaviour, being very careful to show good manners, because they knew that one man, at least, in the restaurant was watching them.

When the meal was over, the elderly man spoke to the twins' parents as they were about to leave. 'Your children look like you, don't they?'

'People do say so,' agreed Mrs MacDonald with a smile.

The twins smiled at the old man. When they were outside Paul said, 'Wasn't that man friendly?'

'Are we really like you?'

'Yes, Sarah, you are,' replied Mrs

MacDonald. 'Children usually take after their parents and often they look very much like them.'

'Yes,' added Mr MacDonald, 'and their hearts take after them too. You may look like me from the outside, but your inside is even more like me. Just as we pass on to you something of what we look like, we also pass on to you sinful hearts. That's why the Bible says that we are all sinners, from the time that we're born.'

The twins were disappointed when they arrived at the beach because the tide was in and the wind was blowing. 'What can we play, Dad?'

Mr MacDonald thought. 'Paul, see that piece of driftwood over there? Bring it here, please, I've thought of a game. But it's a game which we can only play on a part of the beach where there are no people.'

'That's easy,' said Sarah. 'Look! There's no one over there.'

'All right, then, bring that piece of wood.'

The piece of wood was about two feet high. Mr MacDonald pounded it into the sand with a large stone. Then he placed a smaller stone on the top. He then marked out six strides away

31

from the stick and placed another piece of wood on the pebbles.

'Now we take it in turns,' he explained. 'You can pick up any size stones you like from the beach. Then, standing at this piece of wood, you have to try to knock the stone off the stick. Every time you succeed you put a stone on the breakwater so that we know the score. The first person to get ten has won.'

It was great fun, but it took them much longer than they thought. In the end, Mr MacDonald won.

'Do you know, twins, what the word "sin" means?' he asked.

'Is it naughtiness?'

'Well, yes, it is, Sarah, but more than that. It means to fall short of God's standards. It means that even when we try our best we can never succeed in keeping them all the time. What are God's standards or laws?'

'The Ten Commandments,' replied Paul.

'Yes, we've been throwing these stones at the stone on the stick. Sometimes we've managed to hit it, but more often we've missed the mark. The same is true of us and God's laws. There are times when we keep God's laws, but we never keep them perfectly because there are many other times when we break them and that's part of our sin.'

By the time the twins had finished the game, the sun was going down and it was chilly on the beach.

'May we have a game of miniature golf?' asked Sarah.

'That's a good idea,' agreed Mrs MacDonald. 'I could join in too.'

Mrs MacDonald was good at putting. The most amusing moment was when Paul actually got the ball in the hole in one putt. He could hardly believe his eyes and shouted with such excitement that everyone who was playing looked around to see what was happening.

'That was lucky,' grumbled Sarah. Then she thought for a moment. 'It's like knocking the stones off the stick, isn't it, Dad?'

'What do you mean?'

'Well, it's possible to get a ball in a hole with just one shot, but it would be impossible to do it every time.'

'Very good,' agreed her father. 'Can we sometimes keep one of God's laws, Sarah?'

'Yes.'

'Can we keep all of them all of the time?'

'No.'

'Can you think of any law that you've never broken?'

Sarah thought. 'I've kept the commandment, "You shall not murder".'

'Wait a moment,' interrupted Mr MacDonald. 'The Lord Jesus said that we break that commandment if we ever feel like killing someone. Have you ever been angry with someone, Sarah, so that you've felt you really hated that person?'

Sarah sighed. 'Yes, I've felt like that about Paul sometimes, particularly when I've been jealous.'

'Have you ever called anyone names?'

'You know I have,' admitted Sarah.

'Well, the Lord Jesus said that breaks God's law and is sin.'

'But why?' asked Sarah.

'Before anyone kills, he first hates that person; and before he hates, he dislikes that person. The Lord Jesus showed that we've all sinned much more than we realise.'

The twins' mother had finished her last hole. 'Come on, you two,' she called. 'Paul, it's your turn, and then Sarah's.'

While Sarah and her father were preparing to make their putts, Mrs MacDonald took a

35

picture of them.

'Why are you taking a picture, Mum?'

'Can't you guess, Paul?   I took one of the three of you trying to knock the stone off the stick and I'm taking this one of Dad and Sarah putting, to illustrate what sin is, for Dad's talk to the Sunday School.   Sin is like missing the mark.'

4 The Bottle Garden

The twins were very disappointed to wake up on Tuesday morning to find that it was raining again. After breakfast the rain was still pouring down.

'Oh, dear!' complained Sarah, 'I'd looked forward to going out again.'

'Me, too,' said Paul. 'I wanted to play on the beach.'

'Never mind,' said their father. 'There are lots of things we can do. I thought of some before we left home.'

'What then?' asked Sarah excitedly.

'For one thing, I think we'll make a bottle garden.'

'What's a bottle garden, Dad?'

'You get a large bottle, Sarah,' explained Mr MacDonald. 'You put a layer of earth at the bottom and then you place a variety of small plants in the bottle to grow. If you screw the top on, you don't have to water them.'

'Can we do it now, Dad?' urged Paul.

'In a while!' replied Mr MacDonald. 'We must first make a list of the things we'll want. We'll want a bottle - I can get that. Then we'll want some earth or potting compost.'

37

'May I get that, Dad?'

'Yes, Sarah.   There's a hardware store which sells bags of it, near where I'll try to get the bottle.   Potting compost is what you need to ask for.'

'What can I get, Dad?' asked Paul.

'We'll need a few clean stones to put at the bottom of the bottle.   There are some outside, by the side of the cabin.   I think children have brought them up from the sea-shore.   If you put on your raincoat, you could collect a good handful.'

Not long afterward Mr MacDonald drove the car out of the garage, and he and the twins left Mrs MacDonald to tidy up while they were out.   The twins' father managed to buy a fine bottle and Paul and Sarah went together to get the potting compost.

When they met again at the car, Sarah said, 'What about the plants to put in it?'

'We'll find a florist,' explained her father. But they tried without success at two places.   'A better idea,' suggested Mr MacDonald, 'would be for us to try one of the nurseries or garden centres just out in the country.   We've got time.'

The first nursery they came to had no plants

suitable for a bottle garden, except a small begonia which hadn't been sold because it was so small. 'Here, you can have this with my compliments,' said the man in charge. 'It's no use to me, but it will give some colour to your bottle garden.'

They then drove on to a much larger garden centre, and here they found practically every kind of plant that they wanted.

'We'll only be able to get a few in,' explained Mr MacDonald. 'We'll have some tradescantia, a maidenhair fern - not forgetting, of course, our begonia!'

'Will we get all of them into the bottle?' asked Paul, with surprise.

'I hope so,' replied Mr MacDonald. 'We'll have to be very patient and careful.'

When they got home, they set about making the bottle garden. First their father washed the bottle and turned it up on its end to thoroughly dry it out. Then Paul washed the stones he had collected, until they were clean. Sarah spread out the newspaper on the dining table and carried the bag of potting compost in and opened it.

'Now,' explained Mr MacDonald, 'it's very important not to get earth around the inside of

the bottle, because it's difficult to clean it. We'll make a funnel of newspaper, so that the earth goes right to the bottom of the bottle.'

They did this slowly, but it worked well. Then Mr MacDonald took an old teaspoon and fixed it to a long stick, so that he had a kind of gardening spade or fork that would go through the narrow neck of the bottle.

Then the patient business began of planting the different things they had bought, one by one. Paul and Sarah both had a turn, but in the end their father had to complete it, holding in one hand his homemade spade and in the other a thin stick to steady the plants as he lowered them in. They watered the plants, making the water go down the sides of the bottle so that it cleaned it where any earth had touched the sides. He finished by screwing on the top of the bottle.

'Doesn't it look good?' said Sarah.

'Yes,' agreed Paul. 'What do we have to do now?'

'Every day we must turn the bottle around so that every part gets a fair share of the light and the plants will grow and you won't need to water them at all.'

'What shall we do now, Dad?'

'Let's continue talking about what we were discussing yesterday.'

'Okay,' agreed the twins.

'Last time we talked about sin,' began Mr MacDonald. 'What is sin, Sarah?'

'Coming short of the mark.'

'What mark?'

'The Ten Commandments,' answered Paul.

'Let me ask you a hard question now. Why is sin such a dreadful thing?'

Neither Paul nor Sarah answered.

'All right,' continued Mr MacDonald. 'Why doesn't God like sin?'

Still the twins gave no answer.

'Let me try asking you another way,' suggested their father. 'What is God like? What kind of Person is He?'

'He's a good Person,' said Sarah.

'Is sin good?'

'No.'

'Well, God can't like sin then, can He, Sarah?' said Mr MacDonald. 'What else is God like?'

'He's never bad or mean,' said Paul.

'Is sin bad and mean?' asked his father.

'Yes,' replied Paul.

'God can't like sin, then. What else is God

like?'

Sarah remembered a hymn they often sang in church which begins, 'Holy, holy, holy, Lord God Almighty', and so she said, 'Doesn't the Bible say that God is holy?'

'Yes, indeed,' replied Mr MacDonald. 'What do you think "holy" means?'

'I don't know,' said Paul.

'It means to be without sin,' explained Mr MacDonald. 'God hates sin. Will you get me a sheet of paper, please, Sarah?'

Sarah brought a sheet from the desk drawer. Her father laid it on the table and wrote on the left-hand side of the sheet of paper the word God and on the other side the word Us. Then he drew a thick black line between the two words, down the middle of the paper. He wrote at the top of the line the word Sin.

'Sin makes a barrier between God and us,' he explained. 'It comes between us and Him, and God can never be pleased with us while our sin separates us from Him. Can you think of any kind of barrier you've seen today?'

Mr MacDonald had something in mind and Sarah guessed first.

'Yes, I remember, Dad. When we went out shopping this morning we had to go over that level crossing and Paul pointed out the barrier which came down. It was like a large gate which went up in the air when the cars could cross the tracks and came down in front of them when a train passed through.'

'Good,' agreed Mr MacDonald. 'Our sin is like a barrier which comes between God and ourselves, cutting us off from Him. Now the important thing is to understand what God has done to get rid of our sin.'

'We know that,' interrupted Paul.

'All right then, tell us.'

'Jesus died on the cross.'

'Good,' said the twins' father. 'Now watch.'

He drew a line through the centre of the line - the barrier - which represented sin. 'You see what has happened now?'

'Yes,' said Paul. 'You've made that barrier into a cross.'

'I'll explain,' continued Mr MacDonald. 'When the Lord Jesus Christ died upon the cross, He took our sin on Himself. He took the punishment we deserved. He could do this because He was God's own Son who had become a man and had never sinned Himself. If you look at the drawing, the cross has now become a bridge between God and us. If we trust in the Lord Jesus as our Saviour, as the One who bore our sin on the cross, we can come back to God, because our punishment has been taken by the Lord Jesus.'

At this moment Mrs MacDonald arrived home from shopping. 'You look upset, Helen,' exclaimed her husband.

'I am,' she said.

'What's wrong? You haven't had an accident or something?'

'Oh, no. But look, I've got this!' Mrs MacDonald produced a slip of paper which said she had to pay a fine for parking too long at a parking meter.

'How did you park so long at a parking meter, then?' asked Mr MacDonald with surprise. 'You haven't been out much over two hours?'

'It was my fault, all right,' explained his wife. 'I managed to find a parking space, and I was so glad that I'd found a place to park, that I forgot all about putting the money in the meter. When I came back, I found this slip of paper tucked behind the windscreen wiper. I'm so sorry!'

'Don't worry,' said Mr MacDonald. 'I

could do just the same thing. I'll pay it for you.'

'I think you'll have to,' agreed Mrs MacDonald with a smile. 'I've spent all my money shopping!'

The twins and their father laughed. They were glad that she didn't look miserable any longer.

'Now what were we talking about, twins?' asked their father.

'You were talking about Jesus taking our punishment for us and paying the price for our sins.'

'That's a coincidence!' exclaimed Mrs MacDonald.

'What do you mean?' asked Paul.

'Well, that's what Dad has said he'll do for me, isn't it? Dad didn't park the car at a parking meter without paying for it. I did. But because Dad loves me, he's going to pay the fine instead.'

Mr MacDonald nodded. 'Yes, in a far more wonderful way,' he continued, 'that's just what the Lord Jesus did. I deserved to be punished for my sins. The Lord Jesus didn't deserve to be punished, because He never did anything that was wrong. But He paid my debt. Because He paid my debt, God can forgive me and I can go free. God doesn't even remember my sins anymore.'

Mrs MacDonald was listening while she unpacked her shopping. 'It's really wonderful, isn't it, to know that God can forgive us like that, for the Lord Jesus' sake.'

5 Paul Changes His Mind

'What on earth are you two squabbling about?' Mr. MacDonald exclaimed as he came into the dining room.

'Sarah's just hit me,' answered Paul. 'She knows I can't hit her back because she's a girl.'

'You do hit back sometimes,' retorted Sarah.

'I haven't today,' said Paul. 'And anyway you shouldn't hit me.'

'Now stop arguing,' interrupted their father. 'What were you squabbling about, anyway?'

Paul explained. 'I said that I was going to ask you to take us to the beach and Sarah said she wanted to go out into the country. She got angry when I said it was my turn to choose.'

'We can soon end that argument,' commented his father. 'I've decided already where we're going.'

'Where?' asked Sarah with excitement.

'Out into the country to do some blackberry picking.'

'Good,' cried Sarah with pleasure.

'Ugh!' grunted Paul. 'I wanted to go to the sea.'

'It's still rather cold for the sea, Paul,' said Mr. MacDonald, 'and Mum wants to go blackberry picking. If the sun comes out later, we'll go down to the beach this afternoon - I promise.'

He looked at the twins. 'Now, Sarah, are you sorry that you hit Paul?'

'I'm sorry, Dad.'

'Now don't squabble again. I'll just get things ready and back the car out of the garage.'

Mr. MacDonald went to help his wife with the things she had prepared for their day's outing. When he came into the dining room again, he heard the twins arguing again and saw Sarah hit Paul.

'Sarah, why are you hitting Paul again?'

'He's being mean. He says that because I don't like swimming as much as he does, I'm a coward.'

'Did you say that, Paul?'

'Yes.'

'It was silly, wasn't it?'

Paul nodded.

'But Sarah,' continued Mr. MacDonald, 'even though it was silly and unkind of Paul to say that, that was no excuse for your hitting him. And didn't you say that you were sorry about hitting him before?'

'Yes,' said Sarah quietly.

'That means that you weren't really sorry then, Sarah. If you two don't make up soon, I can see we're going to have a miserable day - sun or no sun!'

The twins looked at one another and decided that they would try to forget their squabble.

* * *

They drove up a steep hill to get to the place where the blackberries were to be found. The road twisted and turned.

'Look out!' cried Mrs MacDonald. In front of them were two sheep. They had got out of a field through a hole in the fence. Mr MacDonald tooted his horn and the sheep ran together to the side of the road.

'That's a dangerous place for them to get out,' commented Mr MacDonald as another car passed the MacDonalds, going quickly in the opposite direction.

'I hope the sheep are all right,' said Sarah.

'So do I,' agreed her father. 'The danger in which those sheep find themselves is the picture the Bible gives of us in this world. We're like lost sheep because we've gone astray from God. When we're astray from God, we're in danger.'

Paul hadn't been saying much and his father guessed that he was sulking a little. They found a convenient place to park and Mrs MacDonald gave Sarah a small basket into which she could place her blackberries. She gave Paul a plastic bag, the same as she had brought for her husband and herself.

Paul and Sarah set off further up the hill, along the winding footpath.

'Don't go too far ahead,' Mr. MacDonald called out. 'Mum and I will start down here and we'll catch up with you. We'll bring the picnic basket and we'll have lunch at the top of the hill - that is, if we can wait that long!'

The twins were soon out of sight. For about half an hour their parents saw nothing of them. Then they caught sight of Sarah.

'Hi, Sarah! How have you got on?'

'I've got nearly a basketful.'

'Where's Paul?'

'He went off in a huff, Dad.'

'Not again!'

'He said he wasn't going to pick blackberries. He wanted the basket Mum gave me because it was easier to hold than a plastic

51

bag. I said no because Mum had given it to me.'

'That's right,' agreed Mrs MacDonald.

'He went further up the hill on his own. He said he wasn't going to pick up any blackberries. I told him you wouldn't let him eat any if he did that!'

Mrs MacDonald smiled. 'We had better go and find him.'

They walked up the hill. After about half an hour they reached the top, only to find Paul picking blackberries. He looked sheepish and ashamed.

'Hello, Paul! I understood that you weren't going to pick blackberries.'

'I changed my mind, Dad,' said Paul.

'I told Dad about what you wanted,' said Sarah.

'You're an old tell-tale,' retorted Paul.

'Let's forget all about it,' suggested their mother. 'It's lunchtime.'

At this reminder the twins put aside their quarrels. When they had finished their lunch, Sarah was surprised to see her mother take two pictures of the sky. 'What are you doing that for?'

'I'll explain,' answered Mrs MacDonald. 'You remember Dad talking about what God does with our sins when we trust in the Lord Jesus. I've taken a picture of that cloud on its own over there, and then I've taken a picture of the clear blue sky, so that when Dad talks to the Sunday School about what God does with our sins, he can show these two pictures. When we trust in the Lord Jesus, He blots out our sins like a cloud. He takes them right away.'

Mr. MacDonald listened. 'Does God do this to everyone's sins, twins?'

'No,' said Paul. 'Only those who believe in the Lord Jesus.'

'Is believing the only thing you have to do?'

Paul thought. 'I've heard you say something about us having to repent.'

'That's right,' explained his father. 'When the Lord Jesus first began to preach, He told people to repent and to believe the gospel. What do you think repent means?'

'I'm not sure,' answered Paul.

'It means to change your mind about sin. Supposing a man steals and then he repents, what would you expect him to do?'

'I would expect him to be sorry,' said Paul, 'and to decide not to steal anymore.'

Mr. MacDonald continued, 'You gave us an illustration of changing your mind this morning, Paul.'

'How?' asked Paul. Then he thought for a moment and blushed. 'You mean by saying that I wasn't going to pick blackberries and then deciding to pick them?'

Mr. MacDonald nodded. 'To repent means to be really sorry and to change your mind about the wrong things you've been doing. Instead of continuing in the wrong way, you go the right way.'

'It's always me that does the wrong thing,' complained Paul, looking at Sarah.

'No, it isn't, Paul,' continued his father. 'We all do wrong things. Sarah gave us a good illustration of what repentance isn't.'

'How?' asked Sarah with surprise.

'When I saw you hitting Paul, Sarah, I told you off, and you said that you were sorry. But how do you think I know you weren't really sorry?'

Sarah guessed right away. 'Because I did the same thing again, Dad.'

Mr. MacDonald went on. 'It's important to remember that to repent is to be really sorry, so that you don't want to do the wrong thing anymore. It's quite different from being sorry for yourself because you've been caught doing wrong. Let's see if you know what repentance is, Paul.'

'Well, it means to be really sorry and not to want to do wrong things again.'

'Right. Can you think of things you do that God doesn't like?'

'Hitting one another,' said Sarah. 'And being bossy.'

'Being rude and not thinking about other people,' added Paul.

'Not being helpful at home, and not doing what you and Mum tell us,' suggested Sarah.

'All of those things we can describe as sin,' agreed Mr. MacDonald. 'And they're not very pleasant things, are they? And they don't make you happy. Were you happy when you quarrelled this morning?'

They both shook their heads.

'Did you enjoy your walk up the hill on your own, Paul?'

'I didn't,' admitted Paul. 'I felt miserable, and I was glad when you found me.'

'I'm not surprised,' said Mr. MacDonald. 'Sin makes us feel like that. The Lord Jesus died for our sins. When we change our mind about our sins and are really sorry for them, then God is able to forgive us, because the Lord

Jesus died that our sins might be forgiven. Do you remember the two roads we drew before - the broad and the narrow?'

The twins nodded.

'Well, you can tell which road people are on by the way they behave. If people are always bossy, fighting and disobedient, you may be fairly certain that they're on the broad road. But when we've put our trust in the Lord Jesus and are on the narrow road, we try not to fight and quarrel, and God helps us to think about other people and not just about ourselves. Which road do you want to be on, Paul?'

'On the narrow.'

'And you, Sarah?'

'On the narrow too.'

'Then it's important to remember that you must begin by really being sorry to God about sin and by changing your mind about sin.'

6   Collecting Stamps

That evening, when the dishes had been cleared away, Mr MacDonald said to the twins, 'Have you planned anything special for this evening?'

'No,' replied Paul.   'I've been wondering what we could do.'

'I've something that I think will interest you, that I brought with me from home.'

The twin's father went to his bedroom and came back with a cardboard box.

'What's inside?'

'Wait and see,' he urged in answer to Sarah's question.

'First of all, I'll explain. When I was a boy, perhaps about your age, I started collecting stamps.   When I was older and stopped collecting, I gave a lot away. When Mum and I got married, I nearly gave the rest away, but then I thought I'd keep them in case we had children of our own.'

'Why haven't you shown them to us before?' asked Paul.

'The answer to that question is easy. Although young children may like playing with stamps, they don't always look after them

58

carefully. I think you're both old enough now to find stamps interesting.'

'Oh, yes!' exclaimed Paul. 'Some of the boys in my class collect them.'

'And the girls too,' added Sarah.

'Yes,' continued Paul, 'there's one boy whose dad gets him all the special issues.'

'What we'll do this evening,' explained Mr MacDonald, 'is to sort them out into the various countries, then we'll divide them into two piles, and you can have one each. Tomorrow we'll go out and buy two stamp albums.' He removed the lid from the box and produced some large envelopes bulging with stamps.

'Now this bunch here,' he said, ' is of stamps still stuck on pieces of envelopes. They have come from foreign countries throughout the last few years. Mum and I have put them aside for you. You'll find that there are lots of duplicates, but that won't matter - you can choose the best ones.'

'How do we get them off the envelopes?' asked Sarah.

Mr MacDonald explained that they needed some lukewarm water in a bowl or saucer and that they should allow the paper and stamps to soak until the paper slipped away from the stamps.   Then they had to place them face downwards on newspaper to dry.

The evening just flew by and when their mother said, 'Time for bed, twins,' they groaned and said, 'It isn't late!'

'Look at the time,' suggested Mr MacDonald.   When they looked at the clock they saw that it was half an hour past their bedtime.

'It's not too late for you to talk to us like you always do on holiday?' asked Paul.

The twins' father smiled, not knowing whether Paul really wanted him to talk to them or whether it was that he wanted to stay up late.

'I'll talk to you then and pray with you,' promised Mr MacDonald.

Paul and Sarah washed, undressed, put on their pyjamas and dressing-gowns and came and sat on the couch with their father.   Sarah had her Bible in case they needed it.

On seeing the Bible, her father said, 'Turn, please, to Mark 1, and read verses 14 and 15.'

Sarah began to read, 'After John was put in prison, Jesus went into Galilee, proclaiming the good news of God.   "The time has come," He said, "The kingdom of God is near.   Repent and believe the good news!" '

'Repenting is what we talked about this afternoon, isn't it?' asked Paul.

'Yes,' agreed Mr MacDonald. 'We'll talk this evening for a moment about what it means to believe. The Lord Jesus said that there are two things we must do. We've got to change our minds about sin and we've got to believe. What do you think we've got to believe?'

Sarah thought. 'We've got to believe that Jesus died for us and that He's our Saviour.'

'We've got to believe that He's the Son of God first, though,' interrupted Paul.

'Good,' agreed his father. 'Is that all that believing means?'

'Well, no,' said Sarah slowly.

'What does it mean, then?'

Neither Sarah nor Paul could answer.

Their father went on to explain. 'If I went out and asked a man in the street, "Do you believe that Jesus is God's Son and that He died upon the cross to be the Saviour?" and he answered yes, would that make him a Christian?'

'No,' said Paul thoughtfully.

'Why not?'

'He might not really mean it,' replied Paul.

'But supposing he did mean what he said,

would that make him a Christian?'

'I don't think so,' answered Paul slowly.

'Why not?' his father asked again. When the twins didn't answer, Mr MacDonald said, 'We've not only got to believe that the Lord Jesus is the Son of God, and that He died for us to become our Saviour from sin, but we've to do something about it. Look, supposing I said to you, "The supermarket around the corner is giving away free tennis balls," how would I know if you believed me?'

'That's easy,' said Paul, 'you would know we believed you because we would run round right away to get a tennis ball!'

'That's just how you know someone really believes in the Lord Jesus,' went on Mr MacDonald. 'If you really believe in Him, that He's the only Saviour and that He died for sinners, you'll come to Him and you'll ask Him to be your Saviour.'

'But that's not easy, is it?' asked Sarah. 'We can't see Him, can we? So it's difficult to come to Him.'

'It's true we can't see Him,' agreed her father. 'But He's promised that if we speak to Him - and that's what we do when we pray - He will hear us. If you come to the Lord Jesus, by praying to Him and asking Him to be your Saviour, then you're believing His promise. He promises that if you come to Him like this, wanting to change your mind about sin and wanting Him to save you from your sin, He will hear your prayer.'

'Can we be sure that He hears us, Dad?'

'Yes, Paul. When the Lord Jesus was on earth, He often encouraged people to come to Him and He spoke about prayer. He always hears our prayers. When I ask Him, "Lord, help Paul and Sarah," He hears me as well as when Grandma hears me speaking to her on the phone.'

'Can He listen to everyone who prays to Him all at the same time, Dad?'

'Yes, He can!' explained Mr MacDonald. 'Never forget that the Lord Jesus is God. You believed me about the stamps because I'm your Dad and you know I mean what I say to you. I can believe everything the Lord Jesus says - even though I can't see Him - because He's God. Nothing is impossible for Him. And He can never break a promise. There's a prayer I've often suggested that people can use if they really want to become Christians. Would you like me to tell it to you?'

Paul and Sarah nodded their heads.

'It's quite simple,' their father continued. 'There are three little sentences. I'll say them, then you repeat them after me. Thank you. Come in. Take charge. Can you remember them?'

'Yes,' answered the twins, and they repeated together, 'Thank you. Come in. Take charge.'

'If you really want to become a Christian and you believe in the Lord Jesus, first of all, thank Him for coming into the world to be your Saviour and for being willing to die upon the cross to take the punishment for your sin. Then say to Him, "Come into my life, Lord Jesus, and live within me by Your Spirit." Then say, "Take charge of my life, Lord Jesus, not only now but always." And the Lord Jesus always hears a prayer like that.'

The twins' father drew a picture of a door without any doorknob on it. Then he drew a hand knocking.

'Have you sometimes felt, twins, that it was time you became Christians? Have you sometimes felt that you ought to believe on the Lord Jesus and come to Him and ask Him to be your Saviour?'

Paul and Sarah both nodded their heads.

'And I expect it has been when you've listened to God's Word in Sunday School and in church, hasn't it?'

They nodded again.

'That's the Lord Jesus knocking at the door of your life, wanting to come in, if you will invite Him.'

7   Buying the Stamp Albums

Even before breakfast on Thursday morning Paul and Sarah were sorting out the stamps left over from the night before.

'You are enthusiastic!' exclaimed Mrs MacDonald when she came into the dining room to set the table for breakfast.

'It's fun!' answered Paul. 'And I'm looking forward to getting my stamp album today.'

'Dad's going to take us out this morning to buy them,' added Sarah.

'Is it to be with our pocket money?' asked Paul.

'I don't think so, do you, Mum? At least Dad didn't say so.'

'I think he's going to buy them for you as something extra to your pocket money,' agreed their mother.

Sarah's guess was right, as both she and Paul soon discovered.

'What are the plans for today?' asked Mr MacDonald after breakfast.

'I suggest you go out this morning to buy the stamp albums,' said Mrs MacDonald. 'That will give me a chance to clean up a little, and then I suggest that we have an early lunch and visit the kennels.'

'The kennels?' asked Sarah.

'Yes, the kennels, Sarah,' emphasised her father with a smile.

'Do you mean that we might buy a dog?' asked Sarah, her eyebrows showing her surprise.

'Really, Dad?' cried Paul.

'It all depends,' continued Mr MacDonald. 'We know that you would both like a dog for your birthday. We're not quite sure in our own minds whether we ought to have one or not. But I saw an advertisement in the local newspaper about some kennels quite near to here. I thought we would go and have a look. We don't have to buy one today, but seeing them might help us to make up our minds.'

'Oh, that's wonderful!' cried out Sarah.

'Today's going to be exciting, with both stamp albums and going to the kennels! I wonder what kind of dog we'll have?'

Mrs MacDonald raised her hand in restraint. 'We haven't decided yet whether or not we're going to have one, Paul. And, remember, it isn't your birthday quite yet.'

* * *

When the twins were in the town with their

father, they asked him, 'Where are we going to buy the stamp albums, Dad?'

'Quite a lot of shops sell them, twins. But there's a little place by the station which only sells stamps. I thought we would go there.'

In the window many different stamps were displayed. Paul and Sarah peered at them to see if they had any like them.

The bell rang as they went in. From a little room behind the counter an elderly man emerged with his glasses perched on the end of his nose.

'Good morning,' he said. 'What can I do for you?'

'We would like to buy two stamp albums and some stamp hinges, please,' explained the twins' father.

The old man smiled and looked at Paul and Sarah. 'You're stamp collectors, are you?'

The twins looked at one another. Then they said, 'Yes, we are.'

'You're just starting, are you?'

'That's right - only yesterday.'

'I've just the thing for you,' promised the old man. From under the counter he produced two attractive stamp albums. Each had a map of the world on the front and information to help

the stamp collector identify the stamps of different countries.

After paying for the albums and the stamp hinges, Mr MacDonald took the twins to the public library.

'Why are we going here, Dad?'

'All public libraries have stamp catalogues which you can borrow, Sarah. I've brought the library cards we got last time we were down here at the cabin.'

Paul and Sarah were surprised at how large a book the stamp catalogue was.

Mr MacDonald handed it to Paul and said, 'Would you like to take it to the counter to have the date stamped, please?'

Paul took the catalogue to the counter. The librarian looked at the book and then at Paul. 'You're a stamp collector, are you?'

'Yes,' admitted Paul, a little bashful.

When they got into the car, Paul said, 'It was funny this morning, Dad.'

'What do you mean?'

'Twice I was asked, "Are you a stamp collector?" I hadn't really thought about it before. I had to say yes because I've started to collect stamps. I really feel like a collector now!'

His father thought for a moment. 'That helps us to understand something,' he said.

'What do you mean?' asked Paul.

'Yesterday I spoke to you about how to become a Christian. Can you remember the first thing God wants you to do?'

'You must repent.'

'Yes, Sarah. What else? You tell us, Paul.'

'You must believe that the Lord Jesus is the Son of God and that He died upon the cross for your sins.'

'Is that all, Paul?'

'No, Dad, you must ask Jesus to be your very own Saviour.'

'Good,' commented Mr MacDonald. 'Is there anything else God wants us to do?'

There was silence for a moment.

'I'm sure there is more, Dad, but I can't think what,' said Sarah.

'I'll explain then,' he continued. 'The Lord Jesus said that there is something else we must do. We must let people know what we've done when we've become Christians. How do you think we can let other people know that the Lord Jesus is our Saviour?'

'By telling other people about Him,'

suggested Sarah.

Mr MacDonald reached for a piece of paper from the glove compartment of the car and began to draw. He drew a mouth.

'Yes, you're right. We must be willing to let people know that we've become Christians. We went to buy stamp albums today and then we went into the library to get the stamp catalogue. By the things we were doing people rightly thought that we were stamp collectors. By the things we do and say, we show others whether or not we're Christians. And if people ask a Christian whether or not he trusts in the Lord Jesus, he must be quick to tell them the truth and to explain why he believes in the Lord Jesus. When I became a Christian, I was told that I ought not to be ashamed of letting people know. Do you think it's easy to let people know that you trust in the Lord Jesus?'

'Not really,' said Sarah.

'Why not?'

'You may forget some of the things you ought to do as a Christian.'

Mr MacDonald agreed. 'Yes, if you're just the same as you used to be before you became a Christian, people won't really believe that you've become a Christian.'

Paul thought for a moment. 'Sometimes people may make fun of you if you're a Christian.'

'That reminds me of what Grand-dad told me about the time when he was in the army,' laughed his father.

'Oh, tell us about it,' urged Paul enthusiastically.

'Please,' added Sarah.

'When he joined the army he felt rather nervous about letting people know that he was a Christian. He told me how he can still remember the first night in the barracks. He didn't know if anyone else was a Christian in that room. There must have been about forty men sleeping there. He knew that he shouldn't be ashamed of praying and reading his Bible. He knew he ought to do that night what he would have done at home - that was to kneel by his bed and to pray. He kept on putting it off. He got washed and undressed ready for bed. He looked round to see if anyone else was kneeling.'

'Was anyone?'

'No, Paul. At last he remembered that the Lord Jesus could give him courage and strength. He knelt down by his bed and he prayed.'

'Did anything happen?' asked Paul.

'Yes, it did,' said Mr MacDonald, laughing.

'What?'

'All of a sudden he heard a bang. But he didn't take any notice.'

'What was it?' asked Paul.

'Someone had thrown a boot at his bed to disturb him. He never discovered who threw the boot. Grand-dad told me that he can still remember how very close the Lord Jesus seemed to be to him. And after that it was easy to pray each day and read his Bible. In fact, on the second night, a fellow two beds away from him knelt down and prayed. He told Grand-dad that he had been afraid to do so at first, but when he saw him kneel and pray he knew he must too.'

'I don't think I could do that,' exclaimed Paul.

'Perhaps you couldn't yet,' agreed Mr MacDonald. 'But if you become a Christian, the Lord Jesus said that you must be willing to tell other people about Him and that means that Christians must never be ashamed of letting people know that they are Christians. And if they have the opportunity they must explain what the Lord Jesus has done for them. Do you

75

understand that?'

'Yes,' said Paul and Sarah together.

8   Visit to the Kennels

'I think it will take us about half an hour to get to the kennels,' explained the twins' father as they set off in the car after lunch.

'I'm excited,' said Sarah.

'What about you, Paul?'

'A little bit,' replied Paul, trying not to show that he was really just as excited as Sarah.

After what seemed a very long half hour, they arrived at the kennels, which were at the back of a large country house.   They drove up the drive and rang the front doorbell.

A young girl came to the door.

'May we look at the puppies, please?' asked Mr MacDonald.

'Certainly.   Come this way,' invited the assistant.   She led them through the hall of the house, and then through the corridor to the back of the house.

The doors of the kennels were open.   A piece of wire netting at the bottom of each door stopped the puppies getting out and enabled visitors to see them.

'Oh, look at that puppy!' cried Sarah.

'Which one?'

'That dachshund in with all the other

puppies. What kind are they, Dad?'

'Terriers.'

'Look,' continued Sarah, 'the other puppies are pushing him out of the way. I feel sorry for him. May we have him?'

'We haven't decided yet, Sarah, that we're going to have a puppy,' cautioned Mr MacDonald. 'Let's go and look at the others.'

Paul and Sarah found it fascinating. One of the assistants came up to Mr MacDonald and asked, 'Can I help you, sir?'

'We're just looking around for now, thank you. But can you tell me what the prices are, please?'

'The prices are different according to the breed of the dog,' answered the girl. 'This information sheet gives the prices for the various breeds.'

'Phew!' whistled Paul as he looked at the price list. 'They are a lot of money, aren't they, Dad?'

When the MacDonalds had got back into the car, Mrs MacDonald said to Paul and Sarah, 'What do you think, twins, about having a dog?'

'Before you decide,' interrupted her husband gently, 'it's important to think what it will mean to have a dog. What do you think it will mean if we do have one?'

'We'll have to feed it, Dad.'

'And who will pay for that, Sarah?'

'You and Mum.'

'I guess so,' agreed Mrs MacDonald. 'What else would you have to do?'

'It would have to be taken for walks,' contributed Paul.

'And we would have to train it,' added Sarah.

'And a dog can be a tie,' went on Mrs MacDonald. 'It would be difficult too for us to take a dog away with us on holiday, although I know the same is true of our cat.'

Sarah looked serious and glanced at Paul. 'Should we ask instead for the other thing we thought of for our birthdays, Paul?'

'Do you mean the personal stereos?'

Sarah nodded. 'We had thought about each having a stereo radio recorder as second choice,' explained Sarah. Being twins, Paul and Sarah had their birthdays on the same day and knowing that a dog might not be the right thing, they had thought of something else that they both wanted.

On their way home the MacDonalds went into a radio and television shop and looked

80

around. There was one personal stereo which attracted the twins. 'It's quite a lot of money,' Paul said.

'Yes, but a puppy would cost as much as two of them,' said Mr MacDonald. 'You must think about it and work out what you want to do.'

* * *

That night when it was time for Mr MacDonald to talk to Paul and Sarah before they went to bed, he found Sarah sitting on the couch. She hardly seemed to notice her father as he sat down beside her.

'What are you thinking about, Sarah?'

'I've been thinking about the difference between having a dog and having a personal stereo. A dog would need lots of looking after and frequent walks - and it might be unfair to the cat.'

Paul came in. 'Have you been thinking about what to choose too, Paul?'

'Yes,' he replied. 'I think we ought to choose the personal stereos. It's taken me a long time to decide. I've thought a lot about it. Although I hope we'll be able to have a dog later on.'

'What are you going to talk to us about?' asked Sarah.

'I'm going to talk on what you've been telling me about the dog and the personal stereos,' replied Mr MacDonald.

'What?' asked Paul, surprised.

'The Lord Jesus said,' explained Mr MacDonald, 'that if a man or woman, boy or girl, wants to become a Christian, he or she should sit down and think carefully about it first. A person must count the cost. He or she must understand the difference that it will make and be sure that he or she really wants to become a Christian.'

Sarah interrupted. 'You're saying that becoming a Christian means putting Jesus first.'

Her father nodded. 'It means obeying the Lord Jesus, living your life for Him, and not for yourself. Now, Paul, let's see if you can tell us what you have to do if you want to become a Christian.'

'You have to repent,' answered Paul, 'and believe, and be willing to tell others.'

'Good. Now just watch.'

Mr MacDonald drew some traffic lights. 'God wants you to repent and to believe on the Lord Jesus so that your sins are forgiven and you become His child. And then He wants you to let others know that you belong to the Lord

Jesus so that they may learn to trust in Him too. But don't do any of these things until you've counted the cost, until you understand that if the Lord Jesus is going to be your Saviour, He must be your Master too.'

He coloured in the top light of the traffic lights and wrote 'Stop' by the side.

'You see,' went on Mr MacDonald, 'stop thinking of becoming a Christian until you've counted the cost.'

Then he coloured in the bottom light and wrote 'Go' by the side.

'If you've counted the cost and you understand what it means to be a Christian, there's nothing that need hinder you. God wants you to come to the Lord Jesus and to receive Him into your life as your Saviour and Master.'

The twins' father looked at them.

'You know, twins, I've told you everything that you need to know about becoming a Christian. I think that perhaps God may have been speaking to you. The Lord Jesus has been knocking at the doors of your lives. Now if you really want to become a Christian, I suggest you go away on your own somewhere - perhaps to your bedrooms - and just kneel down and turn these three little sentences that I gave you into a prayer. Do you remember them?'

Paul nodded.

'What were they?'

'Thank you. Come in. Take charge.'

'And then remember,' urged Mr MacDonald, 'you must tell someone. When you've asked the Lord Jesus to be your Saviour, I would like you to tell either Mum or me. Do it on your own. It's no use copying one another. Don't tell one another what you're doing until you've asked the Lord Jesus to be your Saviour.'

9   Second Birthdays

Mr MacDonald was right in thinking that Paul and Sarah felt that God was speaking to them and that the Lord Jesus was knocking at the doors of their lives.

They both went to their bedrooms and knelt down to ask the Lord Jesus to come into their lives to be their Lord and Saviour. Neither knew that the other was doing the same.

When the twins had had time to get into bed, Mr and Mrs MacDonald went into their bedrooms to say goodnight to them.

'Dad,' said Paul, 'I asked the Lord Jesus to be my Saviour tonight.'

Mr MacDonald smiled. 'I'm so glad, Paul. Tell Mum too when she comes in, won't you? Tomorrow morning we'll talk about it.'

When Mrs MacDonald went into Sarah's bedroom, Sarah said to her mother, 'I asked the Lord Jesus to come into my life tonight. Dad said that I should tell you or him.'

'That's wonderful!' exclaimed Mrs MacDonald. 'I've been praying that you would understand that that's what God has been wanting you to do. It's the very best thing we

can do, Sarah. Tell Dad, won't you?'

That night when Mr and Mrs MacDonald prayed together they thanked God for showing Paul and Sarah what they needed to do.

After breakfast the next morning, when Mr MacDonald was about to read the Bible and pray, he said, 'You know, twins, you'll be able to pray now in a different and better way than before. You're Christians now.'

Sarah was wondering how she could be sure she was a Christian. Often in Sunday School she had felt she wanted to ask the Lord Jesus to come into her life.

'How can you really be sure that you're a Christian, Dad?' she asked seriously.

'Let me answer by asking you some questions about our bottle garden,' suggested Mr MacDonald. 'What two things did we need for our bottle garden before we put the plants in?'

'We needed stones and some soil.'

'What two things do we need if we're to become Christians?' continued Mr MacDonald.

'We have to repent and we have to believe in the Lord Jesus, asking Him to be our Saviour,' answered Paul.

'All right,' agreed Mr MacDonald. 'Now, Sarah, going back to the bottle garden. We put in the stones and the soil, and then the plants. How do we know the plants are alive?'

'They've grown.'

'The same will be true of you, Sarah,' explained her father. 'If you've really repented of your sin and believed on the Lord Jesus and asked Him to be your Saviour, you'll now begin to grow as a Christian.'

'What does that mean, Dad?'

'Well, Sarah, you'll want to study the Bible and you'll want to pray. Your life, in the way you behave, will grow more like the Lord Jesus. You'll find that you can't do bad things so easily and that you'll want to do good things. This is because the Holy Spirit is given to us when we become Christians and He gives us strength to do what is right. What's the most interesting thing about keeping a bottle garden?'

'Watching things grow,' answered Paul.

'That's one of the exciting things about becoming a Christian,' went on Mr MacDonald. 'When you become a Christian, you begin to know the Lord Jesus and as you grow up as a Christian you get to know Him more and more. You get to know Him through speaking to Him

88

in prayer and letting Him speak to you as you read the Bible.'

Mrs MacDonald joined in. 'Dad and I will try to help you understand and obey the Bible. Perhaps you'd like to memorize 1 John 5:12-13: "He who has the Son has life; he who does not have the Son of God does not have life. I write these things to you who believe in the name of the Son of God so that you may know that you have eternal life." '

The twins' mother thought of something else. 'Let me ask you a question. Do things grow quickly?'

'No,' they answered together.

'The same is true of us as Christians,' explained Mrs MacDonald. 'Our growing as Christians is often a slow business. But just as you can tell that plants are growing, little by little, so too, we grow as Christians and we can be seen to grow. Do you understand, twins?'

Mr MacDonald joined in again. 'If someone says to me, "I've become a Christian", I'm very glad. I then pray for that person, of course. I also watch that person's life - like watching a plant in our bottle garden. I watch to see if he stops just pleasing himself and tries to please the Lord Jesus. If he does, I know that he's really a Christian.'

This thought worried Paul a bit because he knew that he found it very difficult to be good and well behaved all the time.

'But we can't make ourselves different, can we, Dad?' he asked.

'You're right!' agreed his father with a smile. 'But the Holy Spirit who has come to live in your heart, because the Lord Jesus is your Saviour, can make you strong. Would you like to bring me one of my gloves, Sarah, please?'

It took Sarah a few moments to fetch the glove.

Mr MacDonald put the glove on the table. 'This glove,' he explained, 'can drive a car, carry a suitcase and close a door, but it has to have my hand in it. Your life and mine are like a glove. We can do lots of things if the Lord Jesus lives in us by His Spirit.'

Mr MacDonald had an idea. 'What was yesterday's date?'

'The seventeenth of August, Dad,' answered Paul.

'What I suggest you do then, twins, is that in the front of your Bibles, you write down yesterday's date. Write down not only the day, but also the year, so that you can remember when you became a Christian.   Yesterday was your second birthday.'

'How's that, Dad?' asked Paul with surprise.

'A Christian has two birthdays,' went on Mr MacDonald.   'There was the day he was born into this world and more important still there was the day that he became a Christian, when he was born into God's family.   Now, not everyone can remember when he became a Christian and that doesn't matter, so long as he's sure that the Lord Jesus is his Saviour and Master.   But if you do know the day, it's helpful to write it down, because it's the most important thing ever to have happened to you.'

Bibletime Books

Carine Mackenzie

These are the stories of various Bible characters, accurately retold from the Bible. These books are lively and interesting and are combined with beautifully illustrated pictures.

Old Testament Characters

Esther	- The Brave Queen
Gideon	- Soldier of God
Hannah	- The Mother who Prayed
Jonah	- The Runaway Preacher
Joshua	- The Brave Leader
Nehemiah	- Builder for God
Rebekah	- The Mother of Twins
Ruth	- The Harvest Girl

New Testament Characters

John	- The Baptist
Martha & Mary	- Friends of Jesus
Mary	- Mother of Jesus
Peter	- The Apostle
Peter	- The Fisherman
Simon Peter	- The Disciple

When The Rain Came

Eleanor Watkins

An exciting tale, centring around two boys and their developing friendship. Tom and his family hope to adopt Michael. The family are Christians and Tom has a conscience about his resentful behaviour towards Michael. The main excitement comes during a camping trip, when the boys find themselves left alone one night as the river floods. They attempt to save themselves and the equipment and Michael is almost swept away in the process. Finally, after being rescued they return to the farm where both boys have a sense of belonging; to each other, the family and God.

FULMAR SERIES - 7 to 10 years

The Coal-hole mystery

Teresa Crompton

A pleasant story set in an English village. The main characters are three girls - Amy Stewart (10), a newcomer to the village who becomes friendly with Lisa Ross (10); Sarah Corby (11) is a Christian and lives next door to Amy.

Sarah's and Amy's mothers become friends and they study the Bible together. A mysterious old character called Albert has a coal-hole which he keeps locked. Amy and Lisa are determined to find out what is in the coal-hole. By mischievous and devious means they break in and make an important discovery. Amy struggles with guilt because of the sad consequences of this. Sarah talks to her about Jesus and hleps Amy to explain things to her parents. The situation is resolved and Amy finally has the courage to tell LIsa their actions were wrong.

FULMAR SERIES - 7 to 10 years
ISBN 1 85792 209 3

Arabella Finds Out

Jacqueline Whitehead

Arabella, an oly child, comes from a very wealthy family. She is spoilt and finds it difficult to understand that not everyone is rich. Two village children befriend her, and begin to show her that possessions are not the only valuable things in life. Arabella persuades her paretns to let her go to the local school rather than a private one. She invites her class to her estate, hoping to impress them, but the trip results in a riot. This deepens her friendship with her two new friends and family. She comes to realise that God values a relationship with her and this is something that cannot be bought with money. Just as she begins to feel secure in her new friendships her father makes an announcement which turns the family's life around.

FULMAR SERIES - 7 to 10 years
ISBN 1 85792 161 5